The 1960s
Britain in Pictures

The 1960s
Britain in Pictures

PA Photos

AMMONITE
PRESS

First Published 2008 by
Ammonite Press
an imprint of AE Publications Ltd,
166 High Street, Lewes, East Sussex BN7 1XU

Text copyright Ammonite Press
Images copyright PA Photos
Copyright in the work Ammonite Press

ISBN 978-1-906672-12-6

British Cataloguing in Publication Data. A catalogue
record of this book is available from the British Library.

Editor: Paul Richardson
Picture research: PA Photos
Design: Gravemaker + Scott

Colour reproduction by GMC Reprographics
Printed by Colorprint, China

Page 2: The Beatles,
pictured at EMI House,
Manchester Square, London.
They were presented with
two silver LPs to mark the
quarter-million plus sales of
their first LP 'Please Please
Me' and their new 'With the
Beatles', as well as for their
'Twist & Shout' EP and the
single 'She Loves You'.
28th November, 1963

Page 5: The Millinery
Institute of Great Britain
display part of their Autumn
Collection at Mayfair hotel.
Here, a trio of trouser suits
are worn by June Fry, Jill
Wright and Jenny Wilson.
The hats are from the
Tomboy range.
8th September, 1964

Page 6: Fans waiting in Hyde
Park, London, hours before
a concert by the Rolling
Stones.
5th July, 1969

Introduction

The archives of PA Photos yield a unique insight into Britain's recent past. Thanks to the science of photography we can view the 20th Century more accurately than any that came before, but it is thanks to news photography, and in particular the great news agency that is The Press Association, that we are able now to witness the events that made up life in Britain, not so long ago.

It is easy, looking back, to imagine a past neatly partitioned into clearly defined periods and dominated by landmarks: wars, political upheaval and economic trends. But the archive tells a different story: alongside the major events that constitute formal history are found the smaller things that had equal – if not greater – significance for ordinary people at the time. And while the photographers were working for that moment's news rather than posterity, the camera is an undiscriminating eye that records everything in its view: to modern eyes it is often the backgrounds of these pictures, not their intended subjects, that provide the greatest fascination. Likewise it is revealed that Britain does not pass neatly from one period to another.

The decade between 1st January, 1960 and the 31st December, 1969 was unquestionably the most iconic of the 20th Century. The fashions, music, arts and personalities that emerged then continue to influence Britain more strongly than those of any other period. Given this, photographs of the era portray a world that is more drab than we might imagine, but below the surface everything was changing. This can be seen most clearly in the faces of the young people – and young people come to dominate the news of the time – which wear expressions of challenge and confidence not seen before. This was a generation born after the War, who were experiencing greater affluence and leisure than either their parents' or grandparents' generations: perhaps this explains the decade's explosion of creativity and individualism that fuels Britain still.

Just as Profumo fell before Christine Keeler and Mandy Rice-Davies, so the old order fell before the advance of the new. On the beaches of the South Coast; in Hyde Park; in the universities; on the Isle of Wight, the future had already arrived.

A ladder helps a man and a young girl keep their feet dry along North Parade in the badly flooded town of Worcester, with the River Severn 16 feet above normal level.

25th January, 1960

With the Queen at his
side, President Charles
de Gaulle at a gala ballet
given for him and Madame
de Gaulle – seen talking to
the Duke of Edinburgh (R),
at the Royal Opera House,
Covent Garden, London.
Also pictured are Princess
Margaret (far L) and the
Queen Mother.
7th April, 1960

Princess Margaret and Anthony Armstrong-Jones after the Royal Wedding ceremony at Westminster Abbey.
6th May, 1960

Facing page: Members of the ship's company remove the tampions on the after guns of X and Y turrets on board HMS 'Vanguard' at Portsmouth, Hampshire, in preparation for removing her to the breaker's yard after a 14 year career.
31st May, 1960

The Royal ladies crane forward to view the runners in the paddock before the Derby at Epsom. Left to right: the Queen Mother; the Duchess of Kent; The Queen and the Princess Royal.
1st June, 1960

Facing page: Inside the studios of the British Broadcasting Corporation's £12m Television Centre in Wood Lane, London, believed to be the biggest television headquarters in Europe.
16th June, 1960

Mr Douglas Hoare and his 20 year old daughter Patricia Ann paint a telephone box by the seaside in Swanage, Dorset. The pair work together for the GPO in Hampshire and Dorset, maintaining postal boxes, telephone booths and police boxes.

20th June, 1960

Arsenal goalkeeper Jack Kelsey stops an incredible six shots simultaneously during pre-season training.
16th August, 1960

Lester Piggott tries
desperately to hang on to his
horse, 'Barbary Pirate', as
he is unseated on the final
straight at Brighton.
18th August, 1960

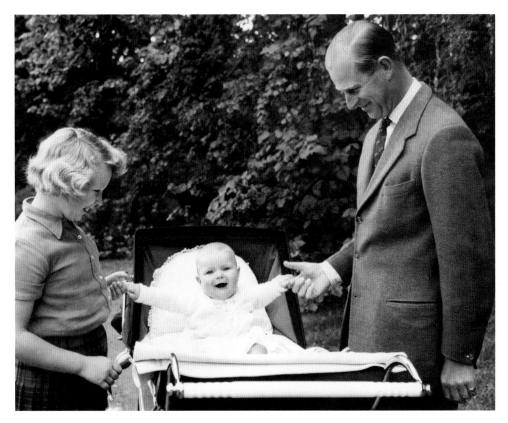

With one hand for his father, the Duke of Edinburgh, and the other for big sister Princess Anne, a laughing Prince Andrew sits up in his pram in the grounds of Balmoral.

8th September, 1960

After being banned for over 30 years, D H Lawrence's book, 'Lady Chatterley's Lover', sells out hours after being released. An Old Bailey jury decided that Penguin were not guilty of publishing an obscene novel, allowing it to be published as it was written.

2nd November, 1960

A double-decker bus ploughs its way through rising floodwaters on the main Newport-Cardiff road in the suburbs of the Welsh capital, following gale-force winds and torrential rain.
4th December, 1960

Mrs Crockwell and her son
David enjoy the Christmas
decorations in their living
room.
17th December, 1960

Chelsea's 17 year old half-back Terry Venables with band leader Joe Loss, rehearsing at the Hammersmith Palais for his debut as a singer.
23rd December, 1960

Arsenal physiotherapist
Bertie Mee using
revolutionary new techniques
to treat an injured patient.
14th April, 1961

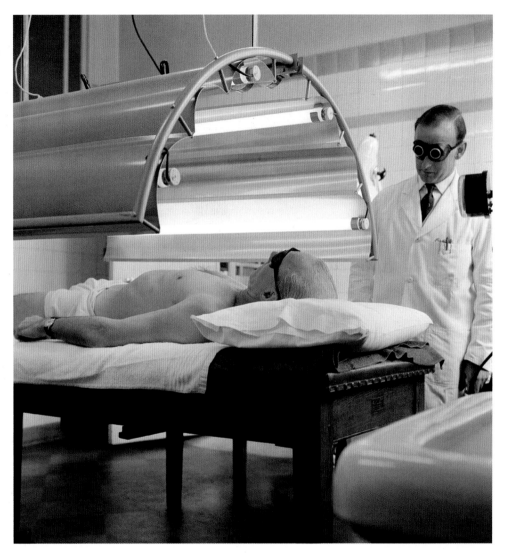

After winning the League championship following a victory over Sheffield Wednesday at White Hart Lane, members of Tottenham Hotspur take a warm bath.

17th April, 1961

Christine Truman and
Angela Mortimer before their
Wimbledon Final.
21st April, 1961

Sculptor and artist Henry
Moore, with his creation
'Stringed Figure, 1938', at the
Tate Gallery in London during a
viewing of six sculptures to be
presented to the Gallery by the
Friends of the Tate Gallery.
28th April, 1961

Tottenham Hotspur players
parade the FA Cup and
League Championship
trophies through London on
an open-topped bus, after
wrapping up The Double by
beating Leicester City 2-0.
6th May, 1961

Comedian Tony Hancock stands stork-like on a chair while manoeuvring his indoor aerial into a good receiving position, in preparation for his new BBC Television series, 'Hancock'.
8th May, 1961

Stirling Moss with the trophy
after his victory in the 200-
mile Silver City Trophy race,
during which he lapped all
but the next two finishers.
3rd June, 1961

American President John Kennedy (R) and his wife Jacqueline (2nd L) pictured with Queen Elizabeth II (2nd R) and the Duke of Edinburgh at Buckingham Palace, in London.
5th June, 1961

Major Yuri Gagarin, the first man in space, waves to bystanders on his departure from Admiralty House, London. With the cosmonaut are seen Mr Harold Macmillan (R) and Mr Aleksander Soldatov (glasses), the Soviet Ambassador in London.
13th July, 1961

Arnold Palmer with
the British Open Golf
Championship trophy at
the Royal Birkdale course,
Southport, Lancashire.
15th July, 1961

Dean Martin (L) and Frank Sinatra (R) make their way across the London Airport tarmac before travelling to Shepperton Studios to film a two minute cameo in Bing Crosby and Bob Hope's comedy, 'Road To Hong Kong'.
4th August, 1961

Cliff Richard and members of his supporting instrumental band The Shadows, at London Airport as they are about to fly off for a Scandinavian tour.
15th August, 1961

Margaret Thatcher takes up her new appointment as Joint Parliamentary Secretary, Minister of Pensions and National Insurance.
12th October, 1961

Facing page: An old horse bus passes the latest London Transport Routemaster in Fleet Street on a drive from Hyde Park Corner to Ludgate Circus for an ITV programme. The run was made to compare the time taken by horse-drawn transport with the journey by motor-bus.
20th October, 1961

England manager Walter Winterbottom (L) examines his team selection: (back row, L-R) Tony Kay, Jimmy Armfield, Bobby Robson, Ron Flowers, Gordon Banks, Ron Springett, Peter Swan, Ray Wilson; (front row, L-R) John Connelly, Bryan Douglas, Ray Pointer, Johnny Haynes, Bobby Charlton.
23rd October, 1961

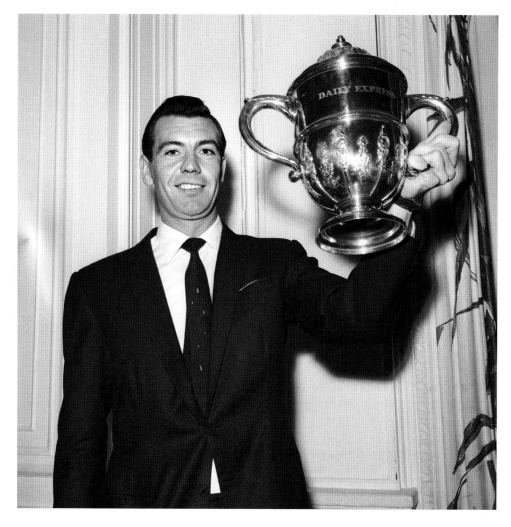

Fulham and England captain Johnny Haynes holds aloft the cup after receiving the Sportsman of the Year trophy at the Savoy Hotel, London.

10th November, 1961

Work started on British United Airways' new passenger terminal at London's Victoria Station. Mr W T Fearne (L), station master at Victoria, and Mr F A Laker, executive director of British United Airways, operate the boring machinery at a ceremony to initiate the foundation work.
13th November, 1961

Bystanders near the gates of Bedford Prison on the day of James Hanratty's execution by hanging as the 'A6 Killer'. The identification leading to his conviction remained controversial until 2001, when DNA evidence from his exhumed body was provided to the Court of Appeal.

4th April, 1962

The Prince of Wales with his father, the Duke of Edinburgh, on his first day at school – Gordonstoun in Scotland. He was greeted by Head Boy Peter Paice (L), Senior Boy Dougal McKenzie with Housemaster Mr R Whitby (3rd L), and Headmaster Mr F R G Chew.
1st May, 1962

Facing page: A new dance, the Apple Twist, demonstrated by Colin and Sidney Wilson at a London party. The Apple Twist is danced to a beat rhythm while the dancers have to keep the apple between their foreheads.
2nd May, 1962

On the far bank of the River Avon stands the Shakespeare Theatre, formerly the Shakespeare Memorial Theatre, opened in 1932 by the Duke of Windsor.

29th May, 1962

Charles Chaplin, wearing academic gown, signs the book at the Encaenia held at Oxford Town Hall upon receiving his honourary degree of Doctor of Letters.
27th June, 1962

A reactor control console inside the nuclear power station at Bradwell-on-Sea, Essex, which was one of the country's first two Magnox reactors that started operation in 1962.
29th August, 1962

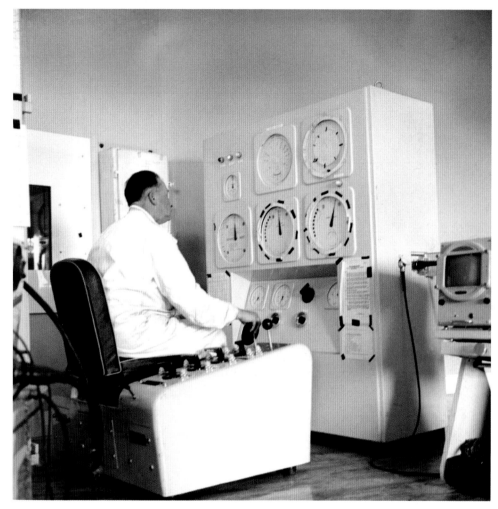

Facing page: Engineers work on the 'Bluebird', which holds the World Land Speed Record.
1st August, 1962

The Hover Rover, an air cushioned, long wheelbase Land Rover.

27th September, 1962

Earl Bertrand Russell, whose cable appeal to Mr Krushchev brought a hint of conciliation in the Cuba crisis, reads in the study of his North Wales home.
25th October, 1962

Margot Fonteyn and Rudolf
Nureyev rehearse 'Le
Corsaire' Pas De Deux at
Covent Garden.
1st November, 1962

Karen Birch lifts the world's smallest car, the Peel P50, off the ground. It weighs a mere 59kg (132lb).
8th November, 1962

Christmas decorations going
up on Oxford Street. A giant
tree is suspended above the
busy thoroughfare.
16th November, 1962

Freddie Mills, Britain's former Light-Heavyweight Champion, is outclassed by George the kangaroo, of the Bertram Mills Circus.
25th November, 1962

A Christmas Party for the 'Not Forgotten Association': 400 men from hospitals and homes were invited. Two dancers from the cabaret show, Connie Reid and Mandy Mather, serve drinks to two of the guests, Bob Struthers and Paddy McCarthy.

13th December, 1962

John Mackenzie tunes in a bell destined for the new Cathedral in Washington DC, USA, at the well-known bell foundry in Whitechapel, London.
19th December, 1962

A security guard guards the office of the Pools Selection Board, as Chairman Lord Brabazon (L), with Board members Ted Drake (C) and Tom Finney (R), work out predictions for the Football League matches cancelled due to the Big Freeze.
26th January, 1963

Singer Cliff Richard listens
carefully to a record on his
radiogram at home.
20th February, 1963

(L-R) 'That Was The Week
That Was' presenters Willie
Rushton, Lance Percival,
Millicent Martin, David Frost
and David Kernan.
21st February, 1963

Lord Beveridge, author of the 1942 Beveridge Report for social security, died at the age of 84 at his Oxford home. Born in Bengal, the son of a civil servant, Lord Beveridge was immensely influential in social economic matters.

17th March, 1963

The New Wembley Stadium.
Improvements include an
electric scoreboard and the
all-encircling roof.
3rd May, 1963

A BBC camera man films through the goal at the European Cup Final – Benfica v AC Milan.
22nd May, 1963

Manchester United captain
Noel Cantwell clowns with
the FA Cup, watched by
teammate Maurice Setters,
as the triumphant United
team begin their journey
back to Manchester after
beating Leicester City 3-1 in
the FA Cup Final.
26th May, 1963

Cassius Clay (later known as Muhammad Ali) takes a breather during an early morning run through Hyde Park, in training for his bout with Henry Cooper.
28th May, 1963

War Minister John Profumo. In a letter of resignation he writes that his 'statement in the House of Commons on March 22nd regarding relations with Miss Christine Keeler, was not true, and misled the Prime Minister and the House of Commons'.

5th June, 1963

Henry Cooper knocks down
Muhammad Ali during the
fourth round.
18th June, 1963

Elizabeth Taylor and Richard
Burton, stars of the film
'Cleopatra', at the ring side
at Wembley, London for
the heavyweight match
between Henry Cooper
and Cassius Clay.
18th June, 1963

Prime Minister Harold Macmillan (R) points out the lie of the land at Birch Grove, his Sussex home, to briefly visiting President John F Kennedy of the United States, during a break in their informal talks.
30th June, 1963

Kim Philby, KGB
and NKVD spy.
1st July, 1963

Christine Keeler (R) and
Mandy Rice-Davies leaving
the Old Bailey after the first
day of the trial of Dr Stephen
Ward, the 50 year old
osteopath, who faces vice
charges.
22nd July, 1963

Under the guidance of police officers, three hooded men are taken to waiting police cars at Linslade, Buckinghamshire, after being remanded in custody on charges in connection with the Great Train Robbery.
16th August, 1963

Facing page: RML 903, one of London's latest and biggest doubledecker Routemaster buses, is swung aboard the Cunard cargo liner 'Alaunia' for a month's visit to Philadelphia, where it will take part in the Exposition Britannia.
12th September, 1963

Sightseers surround French actress Brigitte Bardot as she sits on the back of a bench at Hampstead, London, during a break from the filming of 'An Adorable Idiot'.

25th October, 1963

Bystanders look on during the Tar Barrel Burning Ceremony in Ottery St Mary, Devon.

5th November, 1963

Screaming fans of the pop
group The Beatles, at one of
their concerts in Manchester.
21st November, 1963

Ian Fleming, creator of secret service agent James Bond, during the lunch adjournment of the High Court hearing in which he is being sued for alleged infringement of copyright.
21st November, 1963

Daleks board a London bus,
but are unlikely to travel on
the upper deck.
23rd December, 1963

Arthur Slater, seen behind
the bar of the Red Bull Hotel,
Stockport, Cheshire, where
he has decided to stop
selling cigarettes.
27th January, 1964

Prince Philip, The Duke of Edinburgh, takes a photograph with his Hasselblad camera.
1st February, 1964

State-of-the-art police
vehicles.
9th March, 1964

The Beatles, seated on chairs bearing their names, have their hair worked on by (L-R) Pattie Boyd (later Pattie Harrison, then Clapton), Tina Williams, Pru Berry and Susan Whiteman.
16th March, 1964

Facing page: Supermarket shopping.
19th March, 1964

Honor Blackman (Pussy
Galore) meets Sean
Connery (James Bond)
during a press conference
at Pinewood Studios for the
third Bond film, 'Goldfinger'.
25th March, 1964

Sir Winston Churchill gets an affectionate helping hand from his daughter, Mary, and son-in-law Mr. Christopher Soames, as he leaves their home near Tunbridge Wells. With Lady Churchill, he had been a guest at a family luncheon party to celebrate her 79th birthday.

1st April, 1964

A 15 year old singer from Scotland, Lulu, made her debut with the song 'Shout'.
14th April, 1964

Ronald Biggs, sentenced to
30 years in prison for his role
in the Great Train Robbery.
15th April, 1964

Concert pianist, Joseph Cooper, who is to play at the Bath Festival, poses for an ironic photograph with a dummy keyboard while taking a bath at his home in Surrey.
11th May, 1964

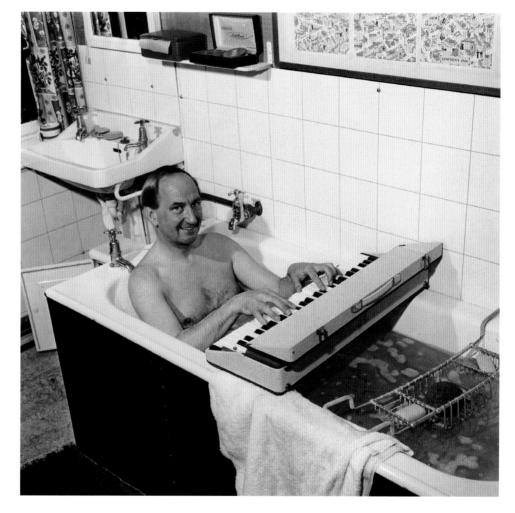

Facing page: Safely through the traffic outside Buckingham Palace, mother duck and the ducklings march on – under police escort – to St James Park and the peace of the lake.
4th May, 1964

Police make arrests during
fighting between mods and
rockers on the beach at
Brighton, Sussex.
18th May, 1964

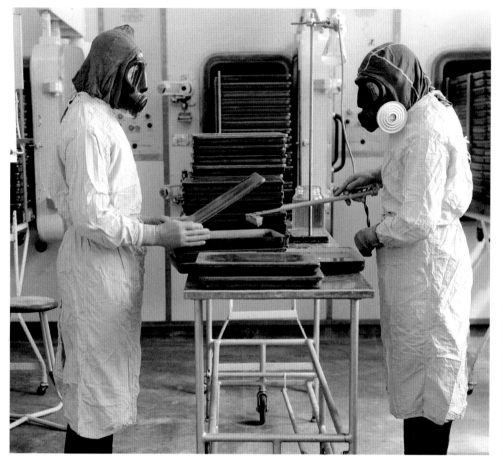

Protected by masks, gloves, overalls and rubber boots, scientists carry out experimental work for an improved anthrax vaccine at the Microbiological Research Establishment at Porton Down, near Salisbury, Wiltshire.

23rd May, 1964

Mods Roy Young and Linda
Jarvis on Derby Sunday on
the Epsom Downs, with their
fully-dressed scooter.
31st May, 1964

Shoppers in the China department of Selfridges store in Oxford Street, London, during the first day of the middle-of-the-year sale in June.
25th June, 1964

Future Liberal Democrats leader Menzies Campbell as a 23 year old Glasgow University law student, crossing the finishing tape to win the 220 yards final at the AAA athletics Championships in London.
23rd July, 1964

Facing page: Top names of showbusiness at the London Palladium in the 'Night of 100 stars'. From left: Susan Hampshire, Anna Massey, Miriam Karlin, Hayley Mills and Barbara Windsor.
5th July, 1964

The Forth Road Bridge opens, spanning the Firth of Forth to connect Edinburgh and Fife and replacing a centuries-old ferry service.
17th August, 1964

Facing page: Teenagers listen to the latest tunes in the Freight Train Coffee Bar.
1st September, 1964

Robert Maxwell, Labour MP
for Buckingham.
1st September, 1964

Facing page: Teenagers
window-shop for records in
Coventry Street, London.
1st September, 1964

Blues and Northern Soul
singer Joe Cocker (R) buys
a copy of his first single, a
cover version of The Beatles'
song, 'I'll Cry Instead'.
1st September, 1964

Amar Singh, the Sikh train guard who was been given permission to wear his turban while on duty on London's Underground, with his wife, Amrid, and their 13 day old daughter, at their Southall, Middlesex home.
2nd September, 1964

The Rolling Stones are banned from the BBC for showing up late for radio shows. From left: Bill Wyman (standing), Keith Richards, front: Mick Jagger, Brian Jones and Charlie Watts.

12th September, 1964

Labour Party leader
Harold Wilson talks into
a microphone during a
campaign tour of London
constituencies.
1st October, 1964

American singing group
The Supremes outside EMI
House in London during a
visit to Britain. From left:
Diana Ross, Mary Wilson
and Florence Ballard.
8th October, 1964

Sir Alec Douglas-Home,
Prime Minister and Leader
of the Conservative Party,
addressing a lunchtime
meeting, mainly composed
of women, in Bedford.
8th October, 1964

England's Terry Venables
practises his splits at
Stamford Bridge in
preparation for the friendly
match against Belgium.
19th October, 1964

Dr. Martin Luther King at the Ritz Hotel, in London on a one-day visit to launch the British publication of his book 'Why We Can't Wait'.
21st October, 1964

The Ford Cortina was voted
the International Car of the
Year, with a top speed of
over 80mph, at the Earls
Court Motor Show.
21st October, 1964

The Queen reads her speech from the throne at the State Opening of Parliament. It was the first time the Queen had opened Parliament with a Labour government.
3rd November, 1964

Carole Ann Ford, who plays Susan in BBC Television's 'Dr Who', autographs a copy of the 'Dalek Book'. She is also demonstrating a child-powered Dalek toy.
28th November, 1964

Manchester United manager
Matt Busby, the first
recipient of the Football
Sword of Honour, presented
to him in Manchester for
'distinguished service to
British and international
football'.
2nd December, 1964

Dr Desmond Morris
introduces Butch the
chimpanzee, from London
Zoo, to children at the Royal
Institute Christmas Lectures.
12th December, 1964

A Leadenhall market
salesman takes a turkey off
the line.
21st December, 1964

Washing hangs over a courtyard between slum tenements in Southwark, South London.
1st January, 1965

Mick Jagger of the Rolling
Stones during filming for
'Ready, Steady, Go'.
1st January, 1965

The Duke of Edinburgh and his son, Prince Andrew, alight from their railway carriage at Liverpool Street Station, London, on return from Sandringham with the Queen and Prince Edward.
27th January, 1965

Facing page: The Kinks perform for the cameras of 'Ready, Steady, Go'.
5th January, 1965

Crowds cram the pavements in silent farewell as the gun carriage bearing the coffin of Sir Winston Churchill is drawn by naval ratings up Ludgate Hill to St. Paul's Cathedral.
30th January, 1965

Facing page: The flag-draped coffin of Sir Winston Churchill is carried to the Port of London Authority launch 'Havengore' at Tower Pier.
30th January, 1965

A queue winds its way through the buildings of the village of Bladon, Oxfordshire, where thousands arrived by car to file silently past the grave of Sir Winston Churchill in Bladon churchyard.
31st January, 1965

Facing page: Alec Issigonis, creator of the British Motor Corporation's 'Mini' car range, drives the 1,000,000th Mini off the production line at the Longbridge, Birmingham, works of Austin.
2nd February, 1965

Malcolm X, leader of the American Black Muslim Sect, after flying back to London. He had been barred from entering France because it was believed his presence might cause demonstrations and trouble. **9th February, 1965**

The Queen Mother wags her
finger at British actor Peter
O'Toole, during a joke in the
foyer of the theatre where
she was attending the Royal
Film Performance.
16th February, 1965

Chelsea goalkeeper Peter
Bonetti makes a flying save
in the semi-final FA Cup
match, Chelsea v. Liverpool.
29th March, 1965

Facing page: Part two of the
Race of Champions gets
underway, as Jim Clark (5),
Dan Gurney (7) and Mike
Spence (6) move off from
the start.
13th March, 1965

Carrying banners, West Country farmers march from Waterloo Station, London, to lobby MPs at the House of Commons before the debate on the farm prices review. 1,200 farmers from Devon, Dorset, Gloucestershire, Somerset and Wiltshire were expected.

31st March, 1965

Groucho Marx enjoys the late evening sun in the Embankment Gardens, London.
31st March, 1965

A view of Fleet Street in
London, looking north
towards the Daily Telegraph
building.
1st April, 1965

James Callaghan,
Chancellor of the Exchequer,
with his brown leather
despatch box which, he said,
symbolised a 'new era'.
1st April, 1965

A BEA Sikorsky helicopter operating from Battersea Heliport made 25 journeys across the Thames to Fulham Power Station, carrying materials needed to replace a gas flue duct on the roof.

5th April, 1965

Facing page: Diana Rigg on a location shoot for a new series of 'The Avengers'. Here she is on a miniature railway near Melton Mowbray, Leicestershire, for an episode entitled 'The Gravediggers'.

4th April, 1965

Paul McCartney, George
Harrison, John Lennon and
Ringo Starr on the ABC
Television 'Eamonn Andrews
Show'.
12th April, 1965

Bank Holiday riots in Brighton. A large crowd of mods gather near the Palace Pier on the beach, a scene repeated a number of times at the Sussex resort, where gangs of mods and rockers clashed during holiday periods.
17th April, 1965

Trafalgar Square, London,
scene of a rally held by
the Campaign for Nuclear
Disarmament after a
three-day march from High
Wycombe, Buckinghamshire.
20th April, 1965

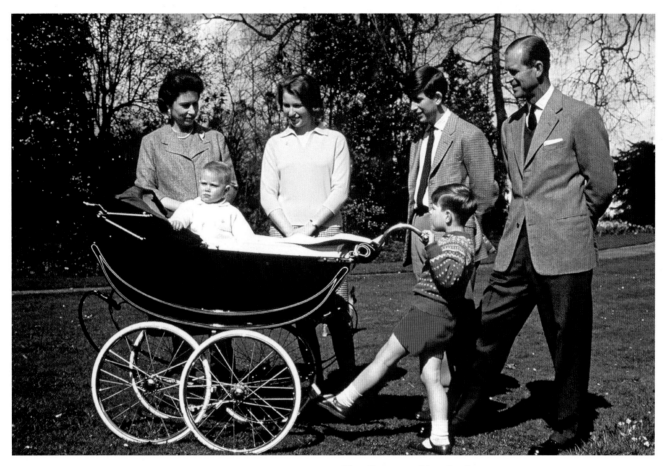

The Queen and her family
at Frogmore on her 39th
birthday.
21st April, 1965

Stoke City's Stanley
Matthews walks out onto
the pitch before the Stanley
Mathews Testimonial Match,
Stoke City v World Stars XI.
28th April, 1965

The 'Flying Scotsman' locomotive leaves Paddington Station, London, at the head of a special train to commemorate the 20th anniversary of VE Day. The train is making a round trip to Gobowen, Shropshire.
9th May, 1965

The Postmaster General, Anthony Wedgwood Benn, demonstrating the new 'Trimphone', the latest deluxe telephone, to be made available as an optional extra in strictly limited quantities in North West London.
10th May, 1965

HRH Queen Elizabeth II
stands at the inauguration
of the John F Kennedy
Memorial with JFK's widow
Jacqueline Kennedy and, to
her left and right, daughter
Caroline and son John Jr.
15th May, 1965

West Ham United celebrate
with the European Cup
Winners Cup after their
2-0 win against TSV 1860
Munich.
19th May, 1965

The Beatles, John Lennon, George Harrison, Ringo Starr and Paul McCartney, almost crowded out by interviewers at a press conference at Twickenham film studios after the announcement that each had received the MBE in the Queen's Birthday Honours.
12th June, 1965

Novelist Kingsley Amis
after his marriage to fellow
novelist Elizabeth Jane
Howard at Marylebone
Register Office, London.
29th June, 1965

Surrey and England batsman
Ken Barrington.
2nd July, 1965

Actor Michael Caine as
'Alfie', with the cast of the
movie of the same name.
4th July, 1965

Peter O'Toole hands Prime Minister Harold Wilson a cup of tea with actor Harry H Corbett (C) at the United Nations Association's garden party at 10 Downing Street.
6th July, 1965

Work continues on the
construction of the new
Victoria Line for the London
Underground.
27th July, 1965

Facing page: Edward Heath
leaving his flat in Albany,
Piccadilly, London.
28th July, 1965

Photographer David
Bailey and French actress
Catherine Deneuve, at St
Pancras Town Hall Registry
Office after their marriage
ceremony.
18th August, 1965

Wilfrid Brambell (R),
who plays Steptoe in the
television show 'Steptoe
and Son', watches Harry
H Corbett (L), who plays
Harold, kiss the bride, played
by Karol Hagar, during
filming at St Luke's Church,
Shepherd's Bush.
2nd September, 1965

Crusoe's Fish and Chip
shop, Uxbridge Road,
London.
9th September, 1965

Lancashire comedian-singer Ken Dodd leaps for joy at the news that his single 'Tears' is top of the New Musical Express Hit Parade. He has just flown in from Liverpool.
20th September, 1965

Members of the cast of 'Z Cars', the BBC television police drama. (L-R) James Ellis (Det Con Lynch), Frank Windsor (Sgt John Watt), Stafford Johns (Chief Inspector Barlow), Joseph Brady (PC Jock Weir), Colin Welland (PC Dave Graham), Robert Keegan (Sgt Blackitt) and Donald Gee (PC Walker).
27th September, 1965

Facing page: View from the balconies overlooking the exhibition stands at Earls Court, London, at the 50th International Motor Show.
1st October, 1965

The Beatles showing
their MBE Insignias at
Buckingham Palace after
receiving them from the
Queen. From left: Ringo
Starr, John Lennon, Paul
McCartney and George
Harrison.
26th October, 1965

The Duke of Edinburgh (R) in uniform as Captain General of the Royal Marines pictured with his uncle, Admiral of the Fleet, Earl Mountbatten of Burma, at the Royal Marines Barracks, Eastney near Portsmouth.
27th October, 1965

The Queen Mother pats her horse 'Irish Rover' after winning the Marden Novices Hurdle.

8th November, 1965

Facing page: The Queen shakes hands with 'Not Only...But Also' star Peter Cook at the Royal Variety Performance at the London Palladium. Cook's diminutive co-star, Dudley Moore, can be seen to Cook's right.

9th November, 1965

Hollywood's Marilyn Monroe is bid a fond farewell by Sir Laurence Olivier and his wife Vivien Leigh at London Airport. Miss Monroe was boarding a Pan American liner with her husband, Arthur Miller, after making 'The Sleeping Prince' with Sir Laurence at Pinewood Studios.
20th November, 1965

London's Trafalgar Square
during a November snow
storm.
22nd November, 1965

The Prince of Wales acting
in the dagger scene as
'Macbeth', in Gordonstoun
School's production of
the Shakespeare play.
The Queen and Duke of
Edinburgh joined other
parents of the boys to watch
the final performance.
30th November, 1965

Comedian Tony Hancock and his bride, publicity agent Miss Freddie Ross, when they married at St. Marylebone Register Office, London.
2nd December, 1965

Opposition leader Edward Heath tries a smoked eel at the International Hotel and Catering Exhibition, Olympia, London.
19th January, 1966

Facing page: Lionel Bart with Barbara Windsor, in a dress rehearsal of 'Twang' at the Shaftesbury Theatre, London.
15th December, 1965

The pirate radio ship 'Radio Caroline' ran aground in rough water between Frinton and Holland on Sea, where she was blown by a gale during the night. Five disc jockeys, taken off by breeches buoy, were among those rescued from the vessel.

20th January, 1966

Model Dian Poore, aged 19, with a selection of Mary Quant handbags and travel bag at the The Leather Fair, Mount Royal Hotel, Marble Arch, London.
7th February, 1966

Stewardess Maureen
Galligan feeds Chi Chi
as the Giant Panda is
transferred from London Zoo
to Moscow to meet An An,
her prospective mate.
8th March, 1966

James Brown signs
autographs on arrival in
London to appear on the
TV pop programme 'Ready,
Steady, Go', before flying on
to Paris.
10th March, 1966

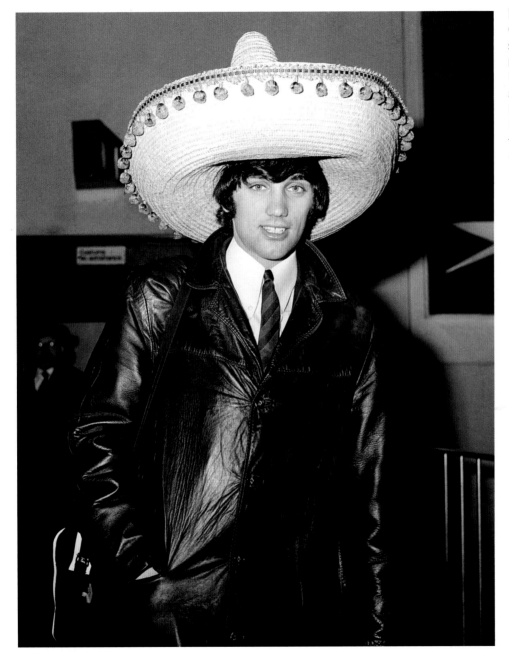

Manchester United footballer George Best wearing a souvenir sombrero on his return to London following United's defeat of Benfica 5-1 in the second leg of the European Cup quarter final. Best scored United's first two goals.

11th March, 1966

Singer Dusty Springfield
at Heathrow Airport before
flying to Brussels for a visit.
22nd March, 1966

Lord Bath (Henry Tynne) raises his hat to one of the lions which will be the star attraction at Longleat Safari Park, two weeks before it opened to the public for the first time.
3rd April, 1966

Patti Boyd in London's West End, showing off a design of the Quorum Autumn Collection, designed by Ossie Clark.
21st April, 1966

Bobby Charlton, Manchester United, Footballer of the Year.
30th April, 1966

Facing page: Film director Alfred Hitchcock at Claridges Hotel. He is there months in advance of his latest and 50th picture, 'Torn Curtain'.
25th April, 1966

Peter Cook (L) and Dudley
Moore rehearsing their
'Leaping Nuns' sketch
for Cook's Revue 'Rustle
of Spring' at the Phoenix
Theatre in London.
2nd May, 1966

Motor enthusiast Peter Sellers performing at the other side of the camera when he was assigned to photograph the Unipower GT Mini.

10th May, 1966

World heavyweight champion Muhammad Ali (formerly known as Cassius Clay) hooded and in heavy boots overtakes a horse drawn brake during early morning training in Hyde Park, in preparation for his title defence against Henry Cooper.
11th May, 1966

Everton players parade the FA Cup around Wembley after their 3-2 win against Sheffield Wednesday. From left: Gordon West, Derek Temple, Mike Trebilcock, Colin Harvey, Alex Young, manager Harry Catterick.
14th May, 1966

Henry Cooper puts his feet up in the sunshine outside the Duchess of Edinburgh Public House in Welling, Kent. With training finished he is relaxing before his great fight for the Heavyweight Championship of the World against Muhammad Ali (Cassius Clay) at the Arsenal Stadium, Highbury.

20th May, 1966

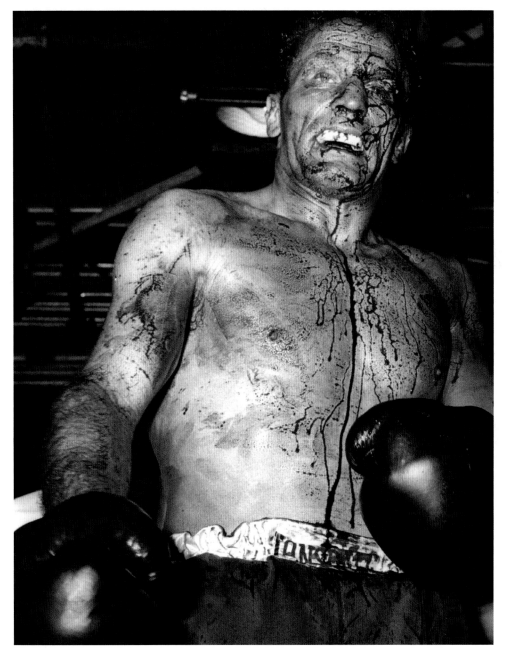

Blood pours from the face of Henry Cooper as the referee stops the World Heavyweight Championship fight in the 6th round. Muhammad Ali (Cassius Clay) retains his title.
21st May, 1966

BBC Commentator Kenneth Wolstenholme kicks off the BBC's coverage of the 1966 World Cup.
31st May, 1966

Facing page: Ascot racegoers, a race in progress and a view of the Heath – the impressive Ascot scene.
1st June, 1966

The Queen Mother talks to
Boer War veterans among
Chelsea Pensioners at their
Founder's Day parade at
the Royal Hospital, Chelsea,
London.
10th June, 1966

The biter bit: famous portrait painter Pietro Annigoni (L) sits for portrait sculptor Anthony Gray at Stamford Bridge Studios, Chelsea, London.
21st June, 1966

New British Open champion
Jack Nicklaus and his wife
Barbara with the trophy,
after Nicklaus won the title at
Muirfield, East Lothian.
9th July, 1966

England's Jimmy Greaves (R) offers some advice to comedian Norman Wisdom (L) on heading the ball when the England World Cup squad visited Pinewood Studios.
12th July, 1966

England captain Bobby Moore holds the Jules Rimet Trophy, collected from the Queen, after leading his team to a 4-2 victory over West Germany, in an exciting World Cup Final that went to extra time at Wembley, London.

30th July, 1966

Nobby Stiles kisses the
treasured World Cup trophy
as Bobby Moore (C) is
congratulated by England
manager Alf Ramsey (in
blue) at Wembley.
30th July, 1966

England's Martin Peters
celebrates scoring his side's
second goal of the World
Cup Final.
30th July, 1966

National flags wave in the crowd during the World Cup Final between England and West Germany at Wembley in London.

30th July, 1966

England World Cup team
Captain Bobby Moore (L)
and World Cup Final goal-
scorers Martin Peters and
Geoff Hurst (R), in their West
Ham United strip.
1st August, 1966

Facing page: Alan Ball of
Everton Football Club, who
supplied the cross from
which Geoff Hurst scored
the controversial third goal,
in extra time, for England in
the World Cup Final.
1st August, 1966

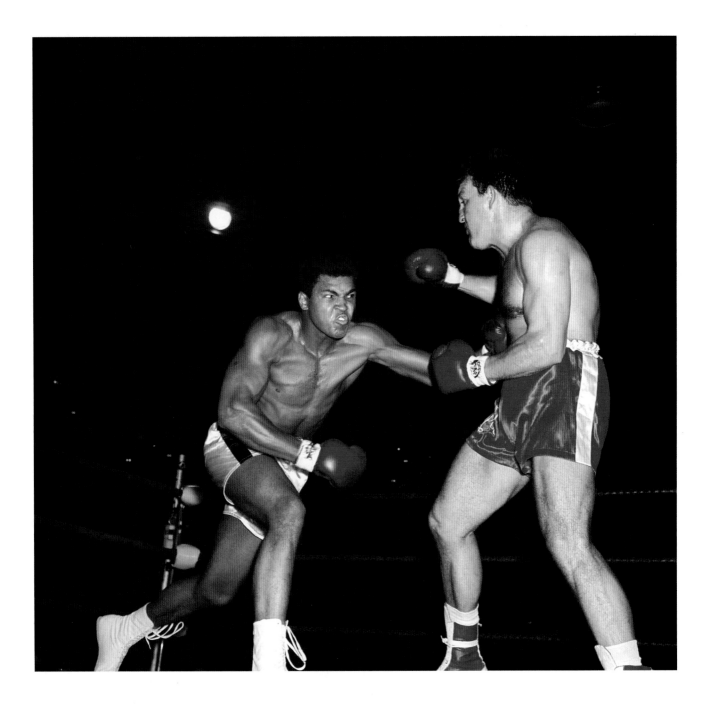

Huge banners draped from the rails of the viewing galleries at the Queen's Building, as hundreds of fans give a loyal send off to the Beatles at London Airport.
11th August, 1966

Facing page: Muhammad Ali catches Brian London with a left to the gut in the World Heavyweight Boxing Championship.
6th August, 1966

Crammed with their luggage into a car, the Beatles are driven across the runway to their aircraft at London Airport, when they left to tour America. Seen through the rain-speckled window are: Paul McCartney, John Lennon, Ringo Starr and George Harrison.
11th August, 1966

England's J Booker rips
around the track in the 8th
British Commonwealth
Games, held in Kingston,
Jamaica.
11th August, 1966

Liverpool manager Bill
Shankly crouches by the
trophies that his team
won the previous season,
including the League
Championship trophy and
the FA Charity Shield, as
his players line up in the
background.
15th August, 1966

A huge concrete cooling tower crumbled under the impact of high winds at Ferrybridge C Power Station near Knottingley, Yorkshire. A report blames errors in the tower's design.

19th August, 1966

The house at 10 Rillington Place in Notting Hill, London, where a series of murders were committed by John Christie in the early 1950s. Timothy Evans, who was wrongly hanged for one of Christie's murders, received a posthumous pardon in October 1966.

12th October, 1966

Facing page: Rescue workers tear into the mud and rubble covering the ruins of houses which, together with Pantglas School, were engulfed by mountain of coal slurry at Aberfan, near Merthyr Tydfil, Glamorganshire, Wales. 144 people, including 116 children, were killed in the disaster.

21st October, 1966

The Queen Mother
meets comedy duo Eric
Morecambe (R), and Ernie
Wise following the Royal
Variety Show.
15th November, 1966

Top-hatted John Lennon of the Beatles stops at the entrance to a public lavatory to chat with Peter Cook. John was playing the part of a commissionaire, hired to give a running commentary about the celebrities using the facilities, part of the 'Not Only But Also' yuletide show.
27th November, 1966

The Beverley Sisters at London Airport when they left for Madrid to appear on Spanish television.
1st December, 1966

Coventry City goalkeeper
Bill Glazier in action at
Molyneux, home of opposing
team Wolverhampton
Wanderers.
3rd December, 1966

The new lightweight Sprite
400 caravan is towed around
London by Margit Saad (R)
and Jean Herbert-Smith to
promote the 10ft, four-berth
vehicle.
4th December, 1966

Facing page: Model Twiggy
on the dodgem cars at
Bertram Mills Circus,
Olympia, London.
1st January, 1967

The moment immediately before the disaster on Coniston Water, in which Donald Campbell died as 'Bluebird' somersaulted at 300mph during a World Speed Record attempt. Campbell's body, and the craft, were not recovered until 36 years later.
4th January, 1967

Tesco, the supermarket chain with more than 500 shops throughout the country, attracted crowds of shoppers when it cut the price of cigarettes.
13th January, 1967

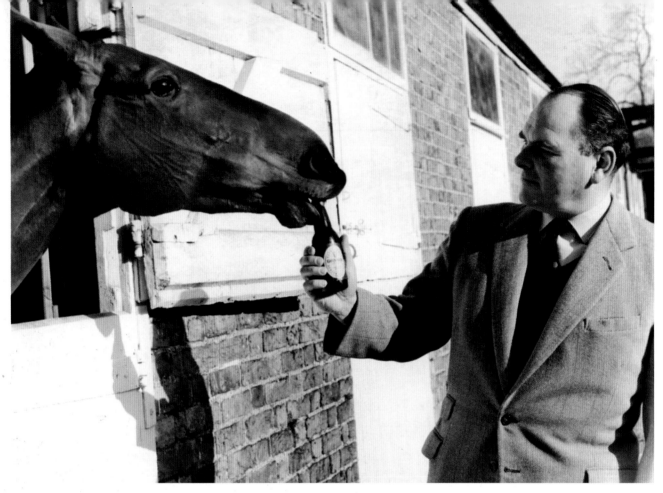

'Arkle', considered the greatest National Hunt horse of all time, enjoys one of his twice-daily bottles of Guinness. Unbeaten in five races during the 1955/56 season, a fractured pedal bone sustained at Kempton Park in December 1966 meant the end of his spectacular career.
20th January, 1967

Cliff Michelmore (L), who is to introduce a BBC2 television programme, 'The Death of Kennedy', is shown with BBC interviewer Kenneth Harris at the Television Centre, Shepherd's Bush, London, inspecting a partly-built 300-square-foot model of Dealey Plaza, Dallas, Texas, USA.

25th January, 1967

A few days after they were arrested for smoking pot, Pop star Mick Jagger of the Rolling Stones and singer Marianne Faithfull arrive at the Royal Opera House in Covent Garden, London, for a Royal Ballet Gala Performance.

23rd February, 1967

Facing page: Margot Fonteyn and Rudolf Nureyev during a rehearsal of Roland Petit's ballet 'Paradise Lost' at Covent Garden in London.

20th February, 1967

The tanker 'Torrey Canyon',
already broken in two on
the Seven Stones Reef, is
battered by waves.
27th March, 1967

Facing page: Start of the
Formula One W D & H O
Wills Trophy at Silverstone,
Northamptonshire.
27th March, 1967

Cat Stevens, later to be
known as Yusef Islam,
backstage at the Finsbury
Park Astoria, London.
31st March, 1967

Alf Kirvin, aged 74, a resident of Archie Street, Salford in Lancashire. The street inspired the setting of television soap opera 'Coronation Street', and was reproduced in the television studios.

15th May, 1967

Facing page: Work in the Picture Transmission Room of The Press Association in Fleet Street, London.
1st June, 1967

The Chelsea Flower Show came to Royal Ascot, Berkshire in the shape of a giant daisy hat worn by Gertrude Shilling, which was designed for her by her eighteen year old son, David Shilling.
20th June, 1967

Lady Diana Spencer (later the Princess of Wales), youngest daughter of Earl Spencer, at Park House, Sandringham, Norfolk with her brother Charles, Viscount Althorp, a former Page of Honour to the Queen.
1st August, 1967

Facing page: Models and a Yorkshire Terrier present creations by the designer Mary Quant in London.
1st August, 1967

Tottenham Hotspur's Jimmy
Greaves plays about with a
camera.
7th August, 1967

Laden with parcels, actor Richard Attenborough is seen with his wife, actress Sheila Sim, and daughters Jane, 12 and Charlotte, 8, after flying into Heathrow Airport, London, on their return from a Mediterranean holiday.
6th September, 1967

The Test

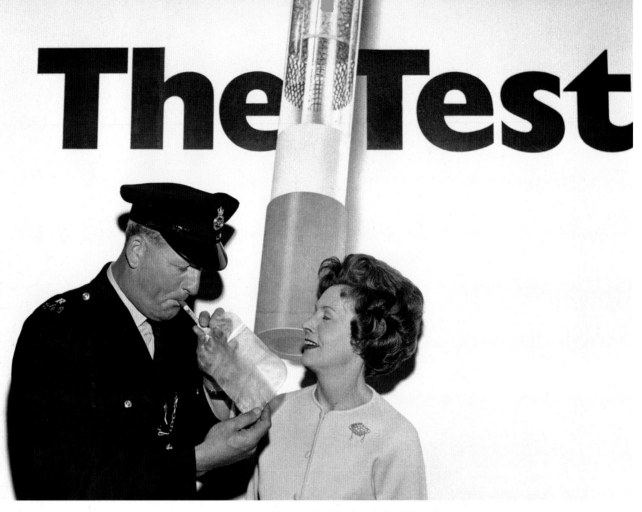

Police Constable Tony Burton of London demonstrating the Alcotest 80 breath-testing device for Mrs Barbara Castle, Minister of Transport, in London where she was launching a drinking and driving publicity campaign to inform the public about the new breathalyser law.
19th September, 1967

'Marquess' provides a real-life lion's roar backing for The Trogs pop group, who were recording the song 'The Lion' in London. The Trogs are (from left) Ronnie Bond, Chris Britton, Reg Presley and Peter Staples.
10th October, 1967

Members of the crew of the frigate HMS 'Wakeful', who took part in the naval escort for the last voyage of the 'Queen Mary', give three cheers as the ship passes by at Southampton.
31st October, 1967

Police keep guard at the entrance to Galn-yr-Afon farm, near Oswestry, when there were several outbreaks of foot and mouth disease in the area.

8th November, 1967

19 year old pop singer Robert Plant (later of Led Zeppelin), from Wolverhampton, visits the office of the Charge d'Affaires of the Republic of China in Portland Place, London, to hand in a letter expressing his interest in the cultural revolution taking place in that country.
15th November, 1967

Facing page: Diana Rigg, star of 'The Avengers' television series.
8th November, 1967

The contestants for the 1967
Miss World beauty title,
photographed at a London
salon having their final 'hair-
do' before the contest.
15th November, 1967

Model Susan Gregg using a new chip vending machine at the Bedford Court Hotel, which serves a fresh portion of chips every 45 seconds at a cost of one shilling.
4th December, 1967

Birmingham City's George Moore and Tommy Bell prepare to paste up a poster advertising the forthcoming fixtures taking place at St Andrew's.
9th February, 1968

Facing page: British pop groups, bound for the USA on a tour which will yield half a million dollars. They are The Jimi Hendrix Experience, Eric Burdon and the Animals, The Alan Price Set and Éire Apparent. The Jimi Hendrix Experience have won a gold disc for their LP, 'Are You Experienced?'.
30th January, 1968

John Hastings, Deputy Master and Controller of the Royal Mint, with the new decimal coinage and its designer, Christopher Ironside.
15th February, 1968

Prince Andrew and Charlie Caroli, the World's Greatest Clown, share a joke over a birthday tea party at the Empire Pool, Wembley, on Charlie's 58th birthday, where he is performing in 'Cinderella on Ice'. The Prince celebrates his eighth birthday in a few days.
15th February, 1968

In her new uniform, Mrs Sislin Fay Allen, who will become Britain's first black policewoman when she finishes her training.
15th February, 1968

Clint Eastwood, newcomer
Ingrid Pitt and British film
stars Mary Ure and Richard
Burton, during filming of a
scene set during World War
II for the film 'Where Eagles
Dare', at Metro-Goldwyn-
Mayer's studios.
16th February, 1968

Leeds United captain Billy
Bremner holds the League
Cup aloft as his teammates
carry him on their shoulders
after their win against
Arsenal.
2nd March, 1968

Legendary Heavyweight boxer Joe Frazier, pictured in London after winning his World title fight with Buster Mathis in New York.
2nd April, 1968

Gerry and Sylvia
Anderson seeing off their
'Thunderbirds' puppets,
bound for Japan, at
Heathrow.
8th April, 1968

The Royal family (L-R) the Duke of Edinburgh, Prince Edward, the Queen, Prince Andrew, Princess Anne and Prince Charles walk by the pond at Frogmore, Windsor.
9th April, 1968

Princess Anne clears the
obstacle fence on her pony
'Purple Star' in the Dressage
event of the Windsor Horse
Trials at Windsor Great Park.
26th April, 1968

West Bromwich Albion
supporters with mascots
at the FA Cup Final with
Everton.
18th May, 1968

David Sadler with the European Cup after Manchester United beat Benfica of Portugal 4-1 in the final at Wembley. He is flanked by team mates Brian Kidd (L) and Pat Crerand.
29th May, 1968

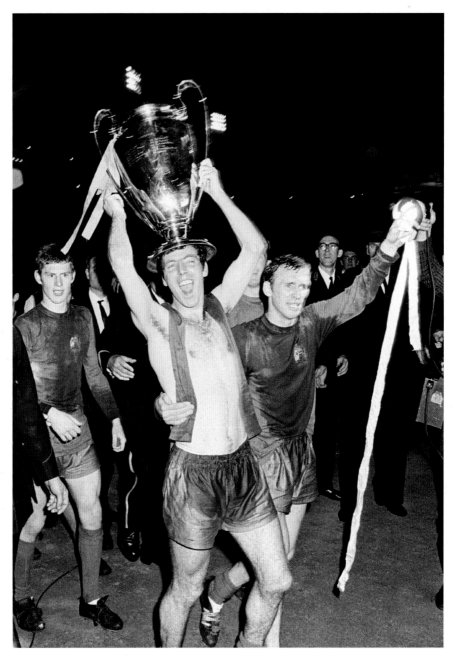

The Queen speaks at the
Trade Union Congress
centenary banquet.
5th June, 1968

Yorkshire skipper Freddie
Trueman takes a well-earned
drink after the county's
victory over Australia at
Bramall Lane, Sheffield.
2nd July, 1968

New Open Golf Champion Gary Player shows his trophy to the crowd at Carnoustie, Angus, Scotland. The 32 year old South African, repeating his 1959 victory, aggregated 289 to win the title. This was two strokes better than the joint runners-up, Jack Nicklaus and Bob Charles.

13th July, 1968

Demonstrators in Grosvenor Square during an anti-Vietnam War march on the US Embassy that followed a rally in Trafalgar Square.
21st July, 1968

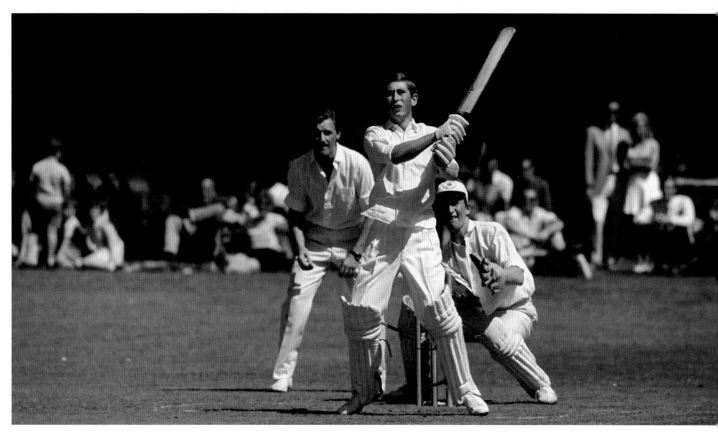

The Prince of Wales batting
for Lord Brabourne's XI
against a team of Grand Prix
drivers at a charity match.
21st July, 1968

Jimmy Savile, BBC Radio One disc jockey.
25th July, 1968

Facing page: Radio One DJs: (back row, L-R) John Peel, David Symonds, Dave Cash, Stuart Henry, Johnny Moran, Alan Freeman; (middle row, L-R) Peter Myers, Mike Ravon, Terry Wogan, Keith Skues, Kenny Everett, Ed Stewart; (front row, L-R) Barry Aldis, Chris Denning, Robin Scott, Tony Blackburn, Sam Costa.
25th July, 1968

Jerry Lee Lewis talks to
guests at a press reception
at the Mayfair Hotel in
London.
8th August, 1968

Athlete Mary Peters (L) competing in the first heat of the 80m hurdles of the Women's Amateur Athletic Association's (AAA) national senior pentathlon, at the Crystal Palace Stadium in London.
9th August, 1968

Eight year old Prince Andrew, the future Duke of York, and his mother Queen Elizabeth II, are greeted on arrival at Heatherdown Preparatory School, Ascot, Berkshire, by headmaster James Edwards and Elizabeth Keeling.

13th September, 1968

The new James Bond,
Australian George Lazenby.
7th October, 1968

Marchers on the Victoria
Embankment after the start
of the great anti-Vietnam
War march in London. An
estimated 20,000 marchers
set off.
27th October, 1968

Facing page: Eli, the baby
elephant, joins pop group
The Who and girls Nicola
Austine (L) and Toni Lee on
a ride on the 'Magic Bus'
from the BBC's Lime Grove
studios, to promote their
latest single.
9th October, 1968

Cliff Richard cuts through the World's Largest Christmas Pudding at the Carlton Tower in London, to be distributed to the Mental Health Trust for patients and hospitals throughout the country.
4th December, 1968

Wreckage of Afghanistan's
Ariana Airline Boeing 727, in
which 50 people were killed
and 15 injured as it crashed
at a fog-bound Gatwick
airport.
5th January, 1969

Enoch Powell MP debates
the immigrant problem with
the Rector of the Church of
St Mary-Le Bow, Cheapside,
in a public meeting.
21st January, 1969

Scottish singer Lulu marries
Maurice Gibb of the pop
group The Bee Gees, at the
Parish Church, Gerrard's
Cross in Buckinghamshire.
18th February, 1969

Australian comedian Barry
Humphries, backstage as
his alter ego Dame Edna
Everage.
12th March, 1969

Beatle Paul McCartney broke millions of teenage girls' hearts when he married his girlfriend Linda Eastman in London.

12th March, 1969

John Trollope and Willie
Penman celebrate Swindon
Town's victory.
15th March, 1969

Facing page: Jackie Stewart
tries his hand at playing
the trombone while sitting
in his Matra Ford, watched
by Chris Barber (R) and his
jazz band.
14th March, 1969

Yehudi Menuhin in
conversation with pupils of
Chetham's Hospital School,
which is to become a junior
school of music.
31st March, 1969

Concorde's maiden flight.
The Anglo-French supersonic
airliner took off on March 2nd
from Toulouse and was in
the air for 27 minutes before
landing. Pictured is Concorde
002, the British prototype,
taking off from Filton, Bristol, on
her 22 minute maiden flight.
9th April, 1969

Newlyweds Roger Moore
and Luisa Mattioli in front of
the press.
11th April, 1969

The Prince of Wales drives
himself to the University
College of Wales, for a nine-
week course, in his MGC
sports car.
21st April, 1969

Round-the-world yachtsman Robin Knox-Johnston aboard his ketch, the 'Suhaili', on arrival in London.
1st May, 1969

Facing page: The MP for Mid-Ulster, Bernadette Devlin, 22, surrounded by schoolchildren in Londonderry.
27th April, 1969

John Lennon, holds Kyoko
Cox, the six year old
daughter of his Japanese
wife, Yoko Ono, on the
child's arrival at Heathrow
airport, where she had flown
in from New York.
18th May, 1969

24 year old disc jockey Kenny Everett with his new bride Audrey Middleton, also known as the singer Lady Lee.

2nd June, 1969

Bob Moncor, Willie McFaul
and John McNamee of
Newcastle United back
home with the European
Inter-Cities Fairs Cup after
beating Ujpesti Dozsa.
12th June, 1969

Facing page: Prince
Charles during his walk and
picnic in Snowdonia after
chairing a Countryside in
1970 committee meeting at
Bangor University.
5th June, 1969

Twisted rails point to a derailed coach of the 14:45 Paignton to Paddington express after the rear four coaches of the train left the track at Skeel Bridge, near Castle Cary, Somerset.
13th June, 1969

Facing page: Mick Taylor (front R) replaces Brian Jones as lead guitarist with The Rolling Stones.
13th June, 1969

Prince Charles and The
Queen Mother walk in
procession after the Knights
of the Garter ceremony at St
George's Chapel, Windsor.
16th June, 1969

Brian Clough, Derby County manager, at the Baseball Ground.

1st July, 1969

The Investiture at
Caernarvon Castle of the
Prince of Wales by his
mother, Britain's Queen
Elizabeth II. There had
been considerable concern
that the ceremony would
be disrupted by Welsh
extremists.
1st July, 1969

Facing page: The Investiture
of Prince Charles as
the Prince of Wales at
Caernarvon Castle.
1st July, 1969

England's Ann Jones stands with her American opponent Billie-Jean King before the start of the Ladies Singles final match at Wimbledon.
7th July, 1969

The day after winning the British Open Golf Championship at Royal Lytham St. Anne's, Tony Jacklin relaxes with his silver trophy beside him in the back garden of his father, a lorry driver who lives near Scunthorpe, Lincolnshire.

13th July, 1969

Police battle with rioters
in the Bogside area of
Londonderry.
14th August, 1969

Facing page: Richard
Branson, organiser of the
Student Advisory Service.
31st July, 1969

People move to and
from the Bogside area of
Londonderry, after a night of
rioting in which at least five
people were shot dead.
15th August, 1969

Astronomer Patrick Moore wearing a souvenir of his visit to the Astronaut's Centre in Houston, Texas, before his BBC Television programme 'Sky at Night'.
17th August, 1969

Bob Dylan in the Isle of
Wight for the island's pop
festival.
27th August, 1969

Facing page: Some 200,000
fans gathered for the Isle of
Wight festival.
31st August, 1969

Author Agatha Christie
celebrates her 90th birthday.
2nd September, 1969

Early arrivals for the last
of the year's free open-air
concerts in Hyde Park.
20th September, 1969

Welsh singer Tom Jones in
the pillared entrance of his
palatial home at St. George's
Hill in Weybridge, Surrey,
on his return to Britain
after almost six months in
America.
27th September, 1969

A convoy of new television detector vans pass over Blackfriars Bridge.
17th October, 1969

Soldiers of the 1st Battalion
of the Parachute Regiment
watch a mixed volleyball
game between girls and
members of the Battalion in
the Morpeth Street area of
Belfast.
25th October, 1969

Stephen Taylor, aged seven, from Chertsey in Surrey, dressed as an astronaut, fixing the top section to an Airfix Apollo Saturn V Rocket Kit.

4th November, 1969

Disc jockey Alan 'Fluff' Freeman spins a disc in his record shop in Leyton.
6th November, 1969

Facing page: Rupert Murdoch looks at one of the first copies of the new 'The Sun' newspaper at The News of the World building in London.
17th November, 1969

Dressing room scene as the
Red Peppers, a variety act
played by Dora Bryan and
Bruce Forsyth, rehearse.
23rd November, 1969

George Best, Manchester United and Northern Ireland soccer star, receiving his award from the Prime Minister Mr Harold Wilson at the Daily Express Sportsman of the Year luncheon at the Savoy Hotel, London.

25th November, 1969

Eton College boys sit on the wall to watch the Wall Game, contested by the Collegers and the Oppidans.

29th November, 1969

Two anti-apartheid
demonstrators who climbed
to the top of the goalposts
during the Springboks match
at Aberdeen.
2nd December, 1969

A Christmas message from John Lennon and Yoko Ono is displayed in Piccadilly Circus, reading 'War Is Over If You Want It'. It is one of 2,000 posters on display in London, and the message also appeared in ten other cities across the world.
15th December, 1969

Facing page: Billingsgate Fish Market in London.
8th December, 1969

Actor and playwright Noel Coward lights a cigarette during his 70th birthday dinner at the Savoy Hotel, London.

16th December, 1969

Mary Whitehouse, General Secretary of National Viewers and Listeners Association, arriving at Buckingham Palace to deliver letters signed by 20,000 people regretting the Queen's decision not to broadcast a Christmas Day message.
22nd December, 1969

The Publishers gratefully acknowledge PA Photos, from whose extensive archive the photographs in this book have been selected. Personal copies of the photographs in this book, and many others, may be ordered online at www.prints.paphotos.com

For more information, please contact:

Ammonite Press

AE Publications Ltd. 166 High Street, Lewes, East Sussex, BN7 1XU, United Kingdom

Tel: 01273 488005 Fax: 01273 402866

www.ae-publications.com